Jim Smiley and His Jumping Frog
and Other Stories

MARK TWAIN

Level 3

Retold by Nancy Taylor
Series Editors: Andy Hopkins and Jocelyn Potter

Pearson Education Limited
Edinburgh Gate, Harlow,
Essex CM20 2JE, England
and Associated Companies throughout the world.

ISBN: 978-1-4058-6239-4

First published by Penguin Books 2005
This edition published 2008

7 9 10 8 6

Text copyright © Penguin Books Ltd 2005
This edition copyright © Pearson Education Ltd 2008
Illustrations copyright © Bob Harvey 2005

Typeset by Graphicraft Ltd, Hong Kong
Set in 11/14pt Bembo
Printed in China
SWTC/06

Published by Pearson Education Ltd in association with
Penguin Books Ltd, a Penguin Random House company.

For a complete list of the titles available in the Penguin Readers series please write to your local
Pearson Longman office or to: Penguin Readers Marketing Department, Pearson Education,
Edinburgh Gate, Harlow, Essex CM20 2JE, England.

Contents

Contents

Introduction

"And what's a frog in a box good for?" asked the man.

"He's good for one thing," said Smiley quietly. "He can jump higher and farther than any frog in Calaveras."

Mark Twain started telling stories when he learned to talk. As the years passed, he became a great storyteller. He wanted to give his readers an amusing trip through a story. The reader and the storyteller share the adventure. You feel that you are in the middle of a conversation with an old friend.

Mark Twain also wanted to give his American readers a true picture of their country and of themselves. He understood how real people think. His stories are funny, but there is a serious side to them, too. Twain wrote about jumping frogs and practical jokes, but also about war, slavery, bad politicians, greedy people, and dishonest governments. He wrote about every important subject of his day.

Mark Twain's real name was Samuel Langhorne Clemens. He was born in 1835 in the state of Missouri. He grew up there in Hannibal on the Mississippi River, with his parents, two brothers, one sister, and Jenny, the family's slave. Jenny was the first great storyteller in the young boy's life.

Clemens began his writing career at an early age. He had to get a job when his father died in 1847. First he worked for a printer, and then he joined his brother at a local newspaper. He started to write short pieces for the paper and enjoyed reading amusing stories about the Wild West by the older writers.

Soon Clemens began to move from state to state. He usually found a job with a printing company or at a newspaper office. After a visit to New Orleans in 1857, he began to work as a pilot on a riverboat. He continued in this job until the American Civil War (1861–65) stopped traffic on the Mississippi River.

In 1861, after a few weeks as a soldier, Clemens traveled with his brother to Nevada. The two young men searched for silver and gold in the Wild West, but Clemens found more success as a writer. In 1863, he started to put a different signature on his writing. On the Mississippi, the pilots shouted "*mark twain*" if the water was deep enough for a big riverboat. Samuel Clemens decided that this was a good name for a writer.

Clemens soon had his first big success using his new name. In 1865, Mark Twain's readers around the country enjoyed his story in the New York *Saturday Press* about Jim Smiley and his jumping frog. From that time, he made his living as a writer and speaker. He traveled around the world, and his books and short stories were very popular during his lifetime.

Mark Twain found information for his writing from his many trips to foreign countries, but most of his stories take place in the United States. His two most famous books, *The Adventures of Tom Sawyer* (1876) and *The Adventures of Huckleberry Finn* (1884), paint an unforgettable picture of the life that he knew as a boy. (You can read these two stories, and *The Prince and the Pauper*, as Penguin Readers.) These exciting and amusing books give the reader a clear idea of life on the Mississippi River in the 1800s. They are very different from a lot of the romantic stories of that time because they are more honest.

Twain had to face some difficult problems toward the end of his life. He lost all of his money in unsuccessful businesses and moved to Europe in 1891. Then he worked very hard to make more money. He gave speeches and wrote cheap mysteries and detective stories. Sadly, his troubles grew worse. His daughter Suzy died in 1896; Olivia, his wife since 1870, died in 1904.

Before his own death, Mark Twain had plenty of money in the bank. He wrote his own life story and started to write amusing short stories and books again. He died in 1910 at Stormfield, his house on a hill in Connecticut.

To many people, Mark Twain is the first writer with a truly American voice. H.L. Mencken, a famous newspaperman, wrote: "I believe that Mark Twain was the true father of our national literature, the first real American artist." Mark Twain's work looks back to a time of spoken storytelling. It covers all kinds of subjects, big and small, and it looks inside people's hearts and minds. It also showed future writers—like Ernest Hemingway and William Faulkner—how to write. Both of these more modern writers tried to copy Mark Twain's honest style. Hemingway described *The Adventures of Huckleberry Finn* as the most important work in American literature.

Mark Twain is still very popular today through his books and also through TV programs and movies of his work. He gave us a picture of Americans: amusing, a bit rough, adventurous, but also trying to be kind, fair, and honest. Twain understood these goals. But, he also knew that people are weak. No one can be good all the time. He was more than an amusing writer—he was also a great teacher. His work helped to shape America's picture of itself.

Jim Smiley and His Jumping Frog

While I was visiting the west coast of this great country, an old friend wrote a letter to me. He made an interesting suggestion:

"You should visit old Simon Wheeler. Ask him about Leonidas W. Smiley. Wheeler won't know Leonidas—he doesn't exist. But when you say the name, he'll remember *Jim* Smiley. Wheeler's got some funny stories about Jim."

I found Simon Wheeler in Angel's Bar in Calaveras, in the north of California, sitting in his favorite chair close to the door. He was asleep, so I had a good look at him. He was a fat old man with no hair on his head but a big white mustache under his nose. He had a simple, kind look on his face.

When Wheeler woke up, I greeted him.

"Good afternoon, Mr. Wheeler. A friend from the east coast has sent me to you for news of his friend, Leonidas W. Smiley."

Simon Wheeler smiled, stood up, and took me to a table in the corner. His chair now blocked the path to the door. I sat and listened silently. No one, I soon realized, could stop Simon Wheeler in the middle of a good story. He never changed his voice as he moved smoothly from one sentence to the next. Did he think the story was serious or funny? He gave his listener no sign. This was his story. You can decide for yourself.

◆

Leonidas W. Smiley, you say? Well, there was a man named *Jim* Smiley here in the winter of 1849. Or, maybe it was the spring of 1850. He was a hard worker and a good talker, but there was something special about him, too. Jim Smiley liked to bet. He was always looking for someone to bet against. He liked to bet on everything: on the weather, on business, and on all kinds of fights and races. He had good luck and almost always won.

His boss's wife had a terrible illness. She was sick for a long time. Then, one morning, the boss came to work with good news.

"How's your wife today?" one man asked.

"She's much better today, thank you," answered the boss. "I hope she'll be well by the end of this week."

Without thinking, Smiley said, "I'll bet five dollars she's dead by Saturday." That's how he was.

At one time, Smiley had a horse. Just for fun, the boys around here called her the fifteen-minute racer because she always walked very slowly. She coughed all the time, and she was old and thin. But she wasn't as slow as those boys thought. For the first half of a race, this horse didn't seem to move. But at the last corner, Smiley's horse came alive. She went crazy and ran like a wild animal to the finish line. She won lots of money for Smiley.

He also had a fighting dog, named Andrew Jackson.* No one liked that dog. He was an ugly little thing. But *he* had a special trick, too. He fought with every dog that Smiley could find for him. He looked weak during the fight. The other dog always bit him and threw him around. Then at the last minute, he turned and got one of the other dog's back legs between his teeth. He could hold on to a back leg all night, or all year.

Andrew Jackson won every fight until one sad day when the other dog in the fight didn't have any back legs! It was the result of an accident in a farmyard. Andrew Jackson didn't know what to do. What could he get his teeth into? He lost the fight, lay down, and died. I always feel sorry when I remember his last night. Jim Smiley loved that little dog.

Smiley had other animals, too. He had fighting chickens and racing birds, and wild cats. Then, one day, he found his best animal: a frog.

* Andrew Jackson: the seventh U.S. president (1829–37)

He noticed this frog when he was fishing. It was looking straight at him. Smiley took the frog home and kept it in his backyard for more than three months. He taught that frog how to jump. Daniel Webster*—that was the frog's name—was the smartest frog along the west coast. Smiley was really proud of Daniel. He said, "This frog can learn anything!" Then he said, "Jump!" and that frog jumped higher and farther than any frog alive. Smiley was always looking for people with frogs. He wanted to bet on Daniel Webster as often as possible.

Smiley kept his frog in a little box with holes along the top. Sometimes he came in here with the box, looking for a bet. One day, a stranger walked into the bar and saw the box.

"What have you got in there?" the man asked.

"Well, maybe it's a cat, or maybe a bird. But, no, it's only a frog," answered Smiley.

"And what's a frog in a box good for?" asked the man.

"He's good for one thing," said Smiley quietly. "He can jump higher and farther than any frog in Calaveras."

The stranger took the box and looked through a hole at Daniel Webster. "It looks like an ordinary frog. I don't see anything special about it."

"Maybe you don't," Smiley said. "Maybe you don't understand frogs. Or, maybe you know a lot about them. I've got my opinion about this frog. I'll bet forty dollars that he can jump better than any frog around here."

The stranger thought about this. Then he said, "I don't have a frog, so I can't take your bet."

"Don't worry. That's no problem," Smiley said. "You hold my box for a minute, and I'll find a frog for you."

The stranger put his forty dollars on the table and took the box. Smiley ran out the door toward the river.

---

* Daniel Webster: a well-known American politician (1782–1852)

The stranger sat in the bar here, thinking. Then he opened the box and got Daniel Webster out. He held the frog's mouth open and poured sand into the animal's stomach.

Soon Smiley returned from the river with a big frog.

"Here's your frog," Smiley said to the stranger. "Put him next to Daniel Webster, and we'll start the race. One—two—three—go!" he shouted, when the frogs were ready.

Both men touched their frogs' backs. The new frog started jumping. But Daniel Webster didn't move. He couldn't move with all that sand inside him. He gave Smiley a sad look.

The new frog won the race, and the stranger picked up the money. As he left the bar, he said, "I still don't see anything special about that frog."

Smiley looked at Daniel Webster. He was surprised and angry. What was the matter? Then he picked his frog up by the neck.

"What's this? Daniel, you're so heavy!"

"Smiley turned the frog over and shook him, and about three cups of sand came out of the frog. When he understood the trick, Smiley was the angriest man in California. He went outside and looked for the stranger, but he was gone. And—"

◆

"Mr. Wheeler!" a boy suddenly called to the old storyteller from the street. "You're wanted at home."

"Stay here," Wheeler said to me. "I'll be back in a second."

I didn't have any reason to stay, so I decided to leave. But at the door, I met Simon Wheeler as he returned to the bar. He started a new story immediately:

"Smiley had a yellow cat with one eye and no tail. This cat's name was Betsy Ross, and—"

But I didn't have time for another story, or any interest in one, so I didn't wait to hear about the cat. I politely said goodbye and left Calaveras.

About three cups of sand came out of the frog.

The Other Side of War

You have probably heard old soldiers' stories about the great things they did in the Civil War.★ Isn't it time to hear about a different kind of soldier? Many young men on both sides went into the war and didn't do anything. Some tried it and returned home almost immediately. Others stayed but saw no action.

In some parts of the country, it was hard for a man to choose his side. Should he fight with the Union soldiers or the Confederates? In December 1860, I was working on a boat on the Mississippi River.

"Have you heard the news?" one of my friends asked. "South Carolina has left the Union."

"That's terrible news," I answered. Like my friend, I was on the side of the Union.

"You're probably happy about it," said my friend. "Your father owned slaves, didn't he?"

"Yes, he did. But he believed slave-owning was wrong. He only had one slave when he died. And that man *chose* to stay with him," I explained.

"Facts are facts. Your father was a slave-owner. You're on the side of the Confederacy," my friend said.

A month later, I met this same friend in New Orleans. By then, I really was on the side of the Confederacy. My friend was, too.

"You can't be on this side," said my friend.

"Why not?" I asked.

"Your father believed slave-owning was wrong," my friend said.

Every week, people found good reasons for changing sides.

★ The Civil War: the war in the United States between the north and the south (1861–65). The northern states wanted to stop the practice of slave-owning. Union soldiers were from the north. Confederate soldiers were from the south.

In the summer of 1861, I was in my hometown of Hannibal, Missouri. Union soldiers pushed into the state and took the three biggest cities. Our local politicians told the men of Missouri to throw out the Union soldiers. About fifteen of my old friends and I formed ourselves into the Hannibal Confederate Company. We wanted to do our part in the war and to protect our state.

Tom Lyman knew nothing about fighting, but he became our leader. Another man, Peterson Dunlap, was a good example of our type of soldier. He was young, intelligent—but didn't know much—and full of romantic ideas. He read books and sang love songs. He was looking for an interesting war with fine uniforms, good weather, and beautiful women waiting for us at the end.

Ed Stevens was another of the soldiers in our company. He was handsome, clean as a cat, and smart as a college professor. But his only goal was to have fun. We had to watch for his practical jokes. The Civil War was a big vacation to him.

Joe Smith was another. He wasn't very smart, in fact he was slow. But he had a warm heart, and he worked hard. He was often homesick, but he was serious about the war. He stayed with the company, and he was killed before the end.

We didn't know anything about war. Tom, Peterson, Ed, and the rest of us were just boys, really. What could a group like us do? Nothing. And that's what we did.

At midnight on our first night as soldiers, we began our walk to the town of New London, about fifteen kilometers away. The first hour was full of fun. We laughed and told stories. In the second hour, the trip seemed like hard work. Everyone was silent, thinking his own thoughts. Then we were near a farmhouse. Our information was that there were Union soldiers in this farmhouse. Lyman gave the orders.

"This is it, boys," he began. "Let's go down there and attack the enemy."

"Are you crazy?" asked Ed Stevens. "I don't want to die. We don't even have any good guns."

"But we're soldiers," said Lyman. "This is our job."

"You can go down there if you want," said Stevens. "Or we can form a circle around the house."

And we did that for the next three hours. Then, when the sun came up, we walked to an open space in the forest.

"That was a good night," said Tom Lyman. "It was our first action as soldiers."

"A great success," agreed everyone.

We began to laugh and enjoy ourselves again. Then we walked to General Ralls's farm, near New London. General Ralls was an old soldier from the Mexican-American War. He gave us a good breakfast and an old-style speech. He spoke about history and love for our country. Now we were ready for anything!

We continued walking to an old building near Jeb Mason's farm. Old Mason and his son were friends of the Confederates. At about noon, a number of farmers arrived. They, too, wanted to help, and they had horses for us and a few guns.

"You can keep the horses until the end of the war," one farmer said. "That'll be in about three months, I think. We'll see you when it ends."

For a few days, we had a good time. We learned to ride the horses in the daytime. Each evening, we visited a farmhouse and were given a good meal. There were often pretty daughters to talk to in the moonlight. Then we returned to our old, empty farm for a good night's sleep. Our life was perfect. Then some farmers came with bad news.

"The enemy is coming this way. They're in New London now. Are you ready for them?"

"Yes, sir," Lyman answered. "We're here to protect you."

After the farmers left, we looked at Lyman. Everyone shouted at the same time.

8

"Are you crazy? I don't want to die."

"How are we going to protect anyone?" "Let's get out of here before the Union soldiers arrive." "Which way should we go?"

"Away from New London," said Lyman. "Let's go back to Jeb Mason's farm. Hurry!"

We ran around like headless chickens and left without our horses. We took our guns and hurried toward Mason's farm. The road was rough with a lot of hills and rocks. One man fell and then the one behind him. We all fell into the river at the bottom of the hill behind the farm. We lost some guns and even a few shoes.

We were very nervous now. Suddenly, we heard a noise. Was it the enemy or a wild animal?

"It has a cough like a wild animal," said Tom Lyman.

We didn't wait to find out. We hurried to Mason's farm as quickly as possible in the dark.

At the farm, three unfriendly dogs ran out to meet us. Each big dog bit into the leg of one of our men and held on tight. We couldn't shoot the dogs without putting our men in danger. For us this was one of the worst actions in the Civil War.

Finally, we saw lights at the farmhouse. Old Mason and his son ran out and threw boiling water on the dogs.

"Where are you going?" asked the old farmer, when we were sitting at his table.

"We don't really know," said Lyman.

"Where are the Union soldiers?" asked the young Mason.

"We don't know that either," Lyman answered.

"You're a strange group of soldiers," said the old man. "Why don't you have a spy to give you information about the enemy? Why are you running around with no purpose? Do you have guards at night? Do you have any idea about war?"

We felt very silly. These farmers knew a lot more about this business than we did. We felt ashamed of ourselves that night when we went to bed. But we weren't in bed for long. At about two o'clock in the morning, we heard the dogs make a terrible noise again. A man on a horse was riding into the yard.

"There's a company of Union soldiers on its way from Hannibal," the man told us. "They're looking for groups of Confederate soldiers like you. They're getting close!"

"Quick!" shouted old Mason. "Get out of the house. One of my slaves will show you a place to hide in the forest."

We ran into the rainy night and followed the slave along a path near the river. By the time we reached our hiding place, we were cold, wet, and scared. It was a wild night, and we all thought about death. This was not the romantic war from Peterson Dunlap's stories.

When the sun came up, the slave returned. "Mr. Mason says the information was wrong. There weren't any Union soldiers near here."

We forgot about death and danger. We were young. Life was full of hope and promise. We hurried back to the farm and enjoyed a big Missouri-style breakfast.

We stayed at Mason's for another week. We town boys got bored with the slow, quiet life of a farm. We were almost happy when we again got news of Union soldiers in the neighborhood. We returned to General Ralls's farm.

Our leader, Tom Lyman, tried to follow some of old Mason's suggestions. "We'll have two guards watching for trouble twenty-four hours a day."

But when night came, no one wanted to be a guard. And nobody wanted to take orders from Tom Lyman. We didn't take orders at home. Why should we take orders here? Finally, Lyman and I agreed to be the guards that night. But we couldn't stay awake after midnight, so we forgot about night-time guards.

Every three or four days, we received more news about the enemy. Usually the message was: "Get ready! Union soldiers are close. Prepare for a fight!"

But we didn't like fighting. When we got these messages, we left. We didn't stay and fight. We ran away. And, usually the news wasn't true. Usually, there *weren't* any Union soldiers in the neighborhood. Soon we didn't take the messages seriously. One night we didn't fight *or* run away. Why should we run? We sat back to enjoy the evening. Then we became nervous. One by one, we went to the window. Were there soldiers out there in the dark? Suddenly, we heard a sound.

"Is anyone out there?" asked one of the young boys.

"I can hear a horse—maybe horses," said Tom Lyman.

"I can see a man near the path. Can you see him?" Ed Stevens asked. "He's on a horse. I think there are other men behind him."

I picked up my gun in the dark. I was shaking with fear. Without thinking, I held my gun up at the window. Behind me someone shouted, "Fire!" I fired my gun. The noise was terrible. Then the man fell from his horse.

"We got him," someone said very quietly.

"Good work," Tom Lyman added. "Wait for the other soldiers to come out of the forest."

We waited and listened. No more soldiers came. There was only silence. After a long time, we went outside and looked at the man. The dead body surprised us. We were sad, too. We looked at him like a friend or a brother. Some of us cried.

"I'm a murderer," I said. "I killed a man. He didn't hurt me. I didn't even know his name."

"I fired my gun, too," said Tom Lyman.

"Me, too," said another man.

Three other men said the same thing. There were six shots fired at the same time. We were all murderers. War was for hard men, and we were just babies. Maybe my gun didn't kill the man, but I *tried* to kill him. I could never fire a gun again.

We learned little about the dead man. He wasn't carrying a gun. He wasn't wearing a soldier's uniform. He probably wasn't a soldier.

"I killed a man. He didn't hurt me. I didn't even know his name."

I dreamed about the dead man. This is what war meant. Soldiers killed strangers. At other times, you helped strangers and they helped you. In a war, you shot them.

I couldn't continue with the Hannibal Confederate Company after this. When our little group had news about a large company of Union soldiers in the neighborhood, about half of us decided to go home. On the road back to Hannibal, we were stopped by General Tom Harris, one of the most important Confederate leaders.

"Where are you men going?" the general asked.

"Home. That's where we belong," I answered.

"You belong here!" General Harris shouted. "You must fight against the Union soldiers. The south must win this war."

"I'm sorry, sir," Tom Lyman said. "We're going home. We killed one man. That's enough. You can kill the rest."

Why have I told you this story? It's a fair picture of the first months of the Civil War. Young men went to war unprepared. Everything was strange and new to them. They often didn't have equipment or uniforms or horses or leaders. They were scared. Some stayed with their companies. They learned how to be soldiers. They ended the war with excellent records, or they were killed. Other men, like me, gave up and went home. I learned how to run away from the enemy. But I didn't learn who the enemy was.

Is He Living or Is He Dead?

In March 1892, I was staying at a quiet hotel in my favorite town on the Mediterranean coast. Mentone has everything: bright sunshine, white beaches, clear blue water. But the very rich don't usually come to Mentone. They like to crowd into Monte Carlo or Nice with other millionaires. Of course, now and then, a rich man does come, and during my stay at the Hôtel des Anglais I met one of these.

At breakfast one morning, my new friend—I will call him Mr. Smith—pointed urgently at the door.

"Quick!" he said. "Look at the man leaving the dining room. Notice everything about him. Do you know who he is?"

"Yes," I answered. "His name is Théophile Magnañ, a rich old man who has been here for about two weeks. He owned most of the cloth factories around Lyon before he stopped working. That's what people say. He never talks to anyone."

After a minute or two of silence, Mr. Smith asked, "Do you know any of Hans Andersen's stories? He's one of my favorite writers."

"Yes, of course," I answered. "Which one are you thinking of?"

"A young boy has a beautiful bird for a pet. He loves the bird but he forgets to feed it. After a time, the bird becomes weak and it stops singing. One morning, the child finds it lying on the floor. His heart breaks. With many tears and sad songs, he places the dead bird in a little box and then puts the box in the ground.

"In the same way, we forget about our great artists when they are alive. We think that they can live on air. Then they die and we spend large amounts of money on their deaths. Why don't we help them when they are alive?"

Later that evening, Mr. Smith and I began to talk again. This is what he told me.

♦

This is a strange story, but a true one. It has been a secret between me and three friends for many years.

A long time ago, when I was a very young artist, I moved from place to place in France. I painted pictures of the beautiful country around me. After some time, I was joined by two other young painters, Claude Frère and Carl Boulander. We loved our work, and we enjoyed living together.

We were very poor, and one day we arrived in a small northern town with no food or money. But we were saved by another young artist. His name was François Millet. He wasn't a famous artist then, of course. He was the same as us. He became the fourth person in our group. We laughed and sang and painted piles of pictures. For two years we lived on a few vegetables each day, but we were happy.

Finally, one day, Claude said, "Boys, we've come to the end. We don't have any money. We have no more vegetables, and nobody will buy our paintings. We need a plan or we will die here with our beautiful work around us."

"It's terrible," said Carl. "Our paintings are good. Some of them—like Millet's *Angelus*—are great, but we don't have any customers for them."

"You can have my *Angelus* for some bread and cheese," said François Millet.

"But wait," said Carl. "I have a plan that will make us rich."

"You're crazy," said Claude. "Lie down until you feel better."

"Be quiet!" said Millet. "Let's hear about Carl's plan."

"OK, think about great artists from the past. When did they become famous? During their lives or after their deaths?"

"Almost always after their deaths," answered Millet.

"So, one of us must die." Carl said this very quietly, so we forgot to jump. But then we pushed him to the ground.

"Listen!" he shouted. "The dead man will become famous. And then all four of us will live as rich men."

"What are you talking about?" asked Claude.

"One of us will stay here and continue to paint," said Carl. "We'll need a great pile of work. The other three will travel around France and tell people about our poor, sick friend. We'll even sell a few of this friend's smaller paintings. People will know his name and begin to talk about him. Then he will die. We'll carry him to his last resting place. We'll make sure that the story is in all of the newspapers. Then everyone will want this dead artist's paintings. Prices will go up and up. We'll be rich for the rest of our lives."

"Maybe three of us will be rich. But one of us will be dead!" shouted Millet.

"No! Don't you see? The man doesn't really die. He changes his name and disappears. We lower an empty box into the ground," Carl explained.

We spent that evening talking about the plan and choosing the dead artist. In the morning, Claude, Carl, and I began our trips around France. François Millet prepared to disappear.

I walked for two days before I stopped on a hill above a large country house. I began to paint a picture of it, and soon the owner came out for a look. He liked my little painting very much. Then I took one of Millet's paintings from my bag.

"I had a good teacher," I explained. "The great François Millet taught me. I am sure you know the signature on this little painting. I shouldn't sell any of his work. He's very sick and won't live much longer. When he dies, you won't get one of his paintings at any price."

Of course, he didn't know François Millet's signature. But suddenly he was sure that he did. After a short discussion, I sold

Millet's painting to him for eight hundred francs.★ When he was "healthy," Millet never got more than five. And, the man bought my picture of his house for another hundred francs. He wanted something by a student of the great Millet. I sent the eight hundred back to François, and then I went to the next town. I sold one picture every day and never tried to sell two.

Carl and Claude followed the same plan in other parts of France. We also talked to newspaper reporters everywhere. In six months, we sold eighty-five small pictures and made 69,000 francs. Carl made the last sale: the *Angelus*, for 2,200 francs. A rich businessman soon bought it again for 550,000 francs. It was time for the great François Millet to die.

Did you read about the death of Millet? Famous people from around the world came to France to say goodbye to him. We four—always together—carried the body in a beautiful wooden box. Only we four touched that box. It didn't weigh much. Of course, we four knew that François Millet wasn't inside it. Millet helped carry the box. On that day, he was a cousin of the famous dead artist. Now, we're all millionaires. If we need more money, we sell another painting. The price of a Millet is very high these days.

♦

"That's a wonderful story," I said when Mr. Smith finished. "But what happened to François Millet?"

"Do you remember when I pointed to a man in the dining room this morning? *That was François Millet,*" Mr. Smith said.

"I don't—" I began.

"Believe it? Yes. It's all true. A great artist was paid for his paintings during his lifetime. He hasn't had to suffer like the little bird in Hans Andersen's story. We made sure of that."

★ francs: old French money

18

We four—always together—carried the body in a beautiful wooden box.

Passport to Russia

It was a bright afternoon in a bar in Berlin. The waiters hurried to the thirsty customers with large glasses of cold German beer. Six American college students were sitting near the entrance.

"But why are you going home now, Parrish?" asked one of the students. "You've only had three days in Berlin. It's the middle of summer. Why don't you stay and see more of Europe?"

"Yes," said another student. "Are you crazy or just homesick?"

Alfred's young face turned red. "I've never been away from home before," he explained. "I haven't seen a friend or had a good conversation for weeks. It's been wonderful to meet you boys. But I don't want to continue my trip alone again after Berlin. I'm going home."

"But you must see St. Petersburg before you return home," one of the students said. His friends agreed.

"Don't talk about St. Petersburg!" Alfred shouted. "I dreamed of seeing that city. But I can't go to another city without a friend." Then he took something from his pocket. "Look. I have my ticket for Paris. I'm going home from there. Let's drink to home and to good friends."

The students ordered more beer.

Finally, the goodbyes were said. Then Alfred Parrish was alone with his ticket and his dreams of home. But he was alone for less than a minute. An older American came to Alfred's table and sat down. He spoke immediately and with great purpose.

"My dear boy, you will be sorry! I heard your conversation with your friends. You must see St. Petersburg. Think about the fine memories you will have. I've known the city for ten years. Everyone in St. Petersburg knows me—Professor Jackson is my name. Even the dogs know me. Promise me that you will go."

Alfred was excited now by the idea of a trip to the Russian city. But then he remembered his other travels.

"I can't. I'm terribly homesick. I won't travel alone again."

"Alone? You won't be alone. I'm going with you," said Professor Jackson.

Alfred was surprised. Things were moving too quickly. Was this a trick? But then he looked at Professor Jackson and saw a friendly, honest face. He decided to believe the older man.

"I can't ask you to do that for me. It's too much trouble," Alfred explained to Professor Jackson.

"No trouble for me, my boy. I'm going to St. Petersburg tonight at nine o'clock. We'll go together!"

But Alfred was ready with another excuse. "It's impossible for me to go to St. Petersburg. I have a ticket for Paris for tonight. I don't have enough money for a train ticket to Russia and a new ticket to France." He placed his last bank note on the table.

In a second, the professor had the tickets and the bank note in his hand. He jumped up.

"Good! Wait here. I'll return in a few minutes. The ticket office will change this for me. They all know me."

Before Alfred could open his mouth, Professor Jackson was hurrying out through the gate.

Alfred Parrish couldn't move. Everything was so sudden. His mouth was open, but his tongue didn't work. His legs refused to move. A stranger had his tickets and his money! He had to get them back. He stood up and began to leave the bar. Then he remembered something. He had to pay for the last six glasses of beer, but he didn't have any money. He didn't speak German, so he couldn't explain his problem to the waiter.

Soon the waiter came over. He picked up the glasses and cleaned the top of the table. At last, he returned to the kitchen. Alfred jumped up and walked quickly toward the door. One step—two steps—three—four—five. Did he hear someone following him? Six steps—seven, and he was out of the bar! He turned the corner. Then a heavy hand fell on his young shoulder.

It was Professor Jackson. "Sorry I took so long. The new man at the ticket office didn't know me. I had to find the boss, my old friend. Here are your new tickets for St. Petersburg. Your suitcases will be on the train. Look, here's a taxi. Jump in, Parrish. To the Russian consulate, driver. As fast as you can."

"Wait!" shouted Alfred. "I have to pay the bill at the bar."

"Don't worry about that. They all know me. I'll pay the bill when I return from Russia," said the professor calmly.

The taxi arrived at the Russian consulate two minutes after closing time. The professor hurried to the door and spoke in Russian to the guard. Alfred couldn't understand a word.

"We need a visa for this young man's passport. Please get it as quickly as possible. We have to catch a train."

"I'm sorry, sir. You need the consul for that. He went home ten minutes ago," said the guard.

"When will he return?" asked the professor.

"Tomorrow morning, sir."

"Oh! But, listen, I'm Professor Jackson. The consul knows me. Everybody knows me. Give us the visa. Tell your boss that it was for me. It'll be all right."

"Sorry, sir. I can't do that," explained the guard.

"Well, then, here is the boy's passport and some money. Put the visa in the passport and mail it to us in St. Petersburg," said the professor, still in Russian.

"You can leave it with me, if you want to. I'll explain the problem to my boss. But, you can't go into Russia without a passport. You should wait until tomorrow," suggested the guard. "There are new rules, sir. If you go into Russia without a passport, the police will put you in prison for ten years."

"Of course they won't! Everybody in St. Petersburg knows me. No problem," said the professor.

"If you go into Russia without a passport, the police will put you in prison for ten years."

On the train to St. Petersburg that evening, Alfred Parrish forgot his worries and enjoyed the professor's amusing conversation. Then, when they were near the Russian border, the young man said, "Professor, could I please have my passport?"

"Oh, sorry, my boy. I left it at the Russian consulate. But they'll send it by mail. You'll get it tomorrow," explained the professor.

"Tomorrow! But I need it now!" shouted Alfred.

"Dear boy, don't worry. The chief of police knows me. The guards at the train station know me. I'll explain everything."

Alfred felt very nervous and very homesick again. When they arrived at the border, Professor Jackson pushed to the front of the line. He returned to Alfred in a few minutes.

"Sorry, my boy. There's a new border guard, and I don't know him."

"Oh, no. I'm finished!" cried Alfred. "It's prison for me."

"Wait. Here's the plan. This new guard wears very thick glasses. I'll cross the border with my passport. Then I'll meet you near the gate and secretly pass it to you. Show my passport to the guard, and you can walk into Russia," the professor said.

"But you're fifty years old. I'm nineteen. The guard will notice," said Alfred.

"The guard can't read the words on a passport. His eyes are too weak for that. He'll wave you through," said the professor.

Ten minutes later, Alfred was shaking badly, but he was in Russia. Soon the two men arrived at their hotel.

"Passports, please," requested the man at the hotel desk.

"Here's my passport," said the professor. "You know me. This young man is with me. Put his name in the book and give him a room. His passport will arrive tomorrow."

The man was very polite, but he was also very serious. He said, in English, "This man cannot stay here without a passport."

"Dear sir, everybody knows me. Just one night. There won't be any problem with that," Professor Jackson said.

"No, sir, it's impossible. I must call the police."

"Stop! Please don't do that. The Chief of the Secret Police will help us. Prince Bossloffsky knows me," said the professor.

Soon the two Americans were in a taxi, racing toward Prince Bossloffsky's palace. The guards stopped them at the door. The prince had guests for dinner, they said. No one could come in at this hour.

"But he'll receive *me*," shouted the professor. "Here's my card. Please send it in to the prince."

After some time, the professor and Alfred Parrish met Prince Bossloffsky in his private office. He was not very patient as he listened to Professor Jackson's request.

"That's not possible," said the prince in perfect English. "Why did you bring this poor boy into Russia without a passport? Are you crazy? He'll get ten years in prison for this."

When he heard these words, Parrish fell onto the sofa behind him. He called for his mother. Tears ran down his face.

"Enough, please," said the prince. "I will give you exactly twenty-four hours to solve this problem. Two of my guards will stay with you until tomorrow at this time. If the boy doesn't have a passport by then, they will take him straight to prison."

The two travelers returned to their hotel rooms, but Alfred Parrish didn't sleep. He wanted to write to his mother before he disappeared into a Russian prison.

My dear Mother,
When this sad letter reaches you, I will be lost in a cold, dark prison in Russia. I met a crazy man in Berlin. He brought me here to Russia and to my problems. In a few hours, the guards will put me in prison. I'm sure that I will die there. There is no hope for me. I can't escape. Please remember me, dear Mother. I love you best of all.

The next day, as the sun went down, the two men and their

25

guards went into the hotel dining room. As they sat down, they heard two English voices.

"Well, we won't get any letters from Berlin tonight."

"Yes, we will. The train had an accident, but it's still coming. It will arrive about three hours late."

"I will die in a Russian prison!" Alfred cried. "Please send my last letter to my dear mother."

"Don't worry, dear boy," Professor Jackson told Alfred. "We'll go to the American Consulate and get a *new* passport for you. We haven't met for years, but the consul knows me."

The consulate was a surprise to the two Americans. It was a small room on the ninth floor of a building in a poor neighborhood. There were two men in the room: the secretary and a typist. The secretary looked surprised when the four men crowded into the little room. Alfred smiled at everyone. He felt safe. This small room was a little corner of America.

The professor shook hands with the secretary and with the typist. Then he asked for a new passport for his friend.

"Sir, I am only the secretary of the consulate. I can't give you a passport. You must see the boss," answered the secretary. "But he is on his summer vacation for the next two weeks."

"We *must* have the passport. In half an hour, these soldiers will throw this poor boy into prison," shouted the professor.

"It's not possible," repeated the secretary. "You know nothing about this young man. You can't prove who he is."

"I am finished!" the boy cried. "This is the last day on Earth for Alfred Parrish!"

The secretary looked at Alfred. "Is that your real name?"

"Yes," said the boy through his tears.

"Where were you born?" asked the secretary.

"In New Haven, Connecticut."

"How long did you live in New Haven?"

"Until I was fourteen years old."

26

"This is the last day on Earth for Alfred Parrish!"

"What street did you live on?" The secretary continued with his questions.

"Parker Street. Why are you asking me these painful questions?" the boy asked. "I'm sad enough without them."

"What kind of house was it?"

"It was made of wood. White, with a dark green door," Alfred answered.

"What could you see from the hall?" the secretary asked.

"A living room on the right and a dining room on the left."

The professor looked at the clock. They only had six minutes. He stood up and blocked the Russian soldiers' view of the clock.

"Were there any pictures on the dining room walls?"

"Just one," answered Alfred.

"What was your father's opinion of the picture?"

The boy's face went red. He was silent for a second.

"Quick. There's no time to lose," said the secretary. "Home or a Russian prison? Your answer will decide your future."

"'It's so ugly. It's the worst picture I've ever seen.' Those were Father's words," nervously reported Alfred.

"Saved!" shouted the secretary, taking a new passport from a pile on his desk. "I know who you are! I lived in that house. I painted that picture!"

"Come here, dear boy!" the professor cried. "This terrible artist and his ugly picture have saved you."

A True Story

It was early on a summer evening. We were sitting outside under one of the big trees near the farmhouse. "Aunt Rachel" was sitting on her old chair next to the children. She was a large, tall black woman. She was sixty years old, but she was still as strong as a woman of twenty-five. She worked hard for us every day. She cooked our meals and cleaned our house. She told stories and sang songs for our children. She was always kind and patient, and she enjoyed a good joke. That evening, she laughed at one of my stories until tears fell from her eyes. I looked at this happy old woman and thought about her past.

"Aunt Rachel," I said, "how have you lived for sixty years without any trouble or pain?"

She stopped smiling. There was a minute of silence, and then she slowly turned her face toward me.

"Have I had any trouble or pain in my life? Mr. Clemens,★ sir, was that a serious question?"

Her quiet voice surprised me. She was not laughing now.

"Well, Aunt Rachel, I've never seen you look sad. You always seem so happy."

"Mr. Clemens, I'm going to tell you my story. Then you can decide," Aunt Rachel began.

◆

My parents were slaves, and I was born a slave, too. We all worked hard, but our farm was a good place. Our owner was an honest woman, named Mrs. O'Hara. At eighteen, I married my husband. He was a slave on Mrs. O'Hara's farm, too. He was a big, strong, handsome man. He was as loving and kind to me and our seven

★ Mr. Samuel Clemens: Mark Twain's real name

children as you are to your family. We wanted to watch those children grow up.

Well, sir, I was born in Virginia, but my mother was from Maryland. When she was angry, Mama was frightening. She always shook her finger at us and said, "I wasn't born in Virginia. You can't tell *me* about life. I'm one of the old Blue Chickens from Maryland, and don't forget it!" People from Maryland call themselves old Blue Chickens, and they're proud of it.

One day, my youngest child fell and cut his arm and his head very badly. A lot of slaves hurried into our kitchen. They wanted to help little Henry. Then my mother arrived and saw the crowd.

"Listen!" she shouted. "I wasn't born in Virginia. I'm one of the old Blue Chickens from Maryland. Now, leave my kitchen. You aren't needed. *I* will be my grandson's nurse."

Well, time passed and one day Mrs. O'Hara said, "I've lost all of my money. I have to sell the farm and my slaves."

We were sent to Richmond in chains. We stood on a stage outside in the hot sun. Crowds of people came and looked at us. They felt our arms and legs and looked at our teeth. My husband was young and strong. He was sold very quickly and disappeared into the crowd with his new owner. Then, one by one, my children were sold. When I began to cry, a white man hit me. Six of my children were gone, but I was holding little Henry's hand.

"Don't take my little boy," I cried to the white men. "I'll kill you if you take him."

But my little Henry said very quietly in my ear, "Don't worry, Mama. I'm going to escape. I'll come back and buy you one day. We'll both be free."

Henry was a good child. He always helped me and my husband, but I couldn't protect him. They pulled him away from me. I tried to stop them. I hit the white men with my chains, but they carried my youngest child away.

My husband and my seven children were gone. Finally,

"Don't take my little boy," I cried to the white men.

Mr. Jefferson from the coast of Virginia bought me. That was twenty-two years ago last Christmas. I worked as a cook for the Jefferson family for a number of years. Then the Civil War came, and the soldiers from the north took the big house and farm. Mr. Jefferson and his family disappeared the night before the soldiers arrived. They left their slaves behind.

The Union officers moved into the house, and one of them said, "Will you cook for us?"

"Yes, sir, I will," I answered. "That's my job."

The officer wasn't a regular soldier. He was an important officer, a general. He said, "Thank you very much. Now you're the boss in this kitchen. If you have any problems, come to me. You're with friends now."

Those officers were very kind, polite men. One day, I felt brave. I decided to talk to them about my little Henry. Maybe he escaped from his owner and went to the north. I explained everything to the officers, and they listened to me very politely.

Finally I said, "Have you seen my little boy? He had a bad cut on his arm and on his head."

Then the general looked worried. He said, "Mrs. Rachel, when did you last see your boy?"

"About thirteen years ago," I said.

"He isn't a boy now. He's a man," explained the general.

"I never thought of that before. You're right, of course. This year he will be twenty years old!" Sadly, none of the officers knew anything about my Henry.

I didn't know it at the time, but Henry's story was a good one. He did escape from his owner and travel to the north. He cut men's hair in a little shop for a number of years. Then one day, he said to himself, "I'm finished with this easy life. I'm going to find my mother if she isn't dead."

So Henry became a soldier and went to work for some of the Union officers. He traveled with the soldiers and looked everywhere for me, his old mother. But I didn't know anything about his search. How could I know?

Then one night at the Jefferson house, we had a big party for some black soldiers. A party meant a lot of work for me. The young men were always hungry and thirsty. They were usually loud, and they danced all night.

That night, the soldiers were having a fine time. One young black man looked more handsome than all the others. He danced beautifully with the prettiest girl in the room. Everyone watched them. When they were close to me, the young man greeted me. Then he said something nice about my red hat.

"Dance with that pretty lady and be quiet," I said with a smile.

I saw the young man's face change suddenly, just for a second. Then he joined the other dancers again.

Later in the evening, another crowd of soldiers arrived. There were too many people for the house, and I was angry.

"Listen!" I shouted. "I want you boys to understand something. You've had a good time, but now I've had enough of you. You've eaten all the food in my kitchen, and you've made a big mess. I'm one of the old Blue Chickens from Maryland, and don't forget it! Now, this party is at an end."

The handsome young man stopped dancing. He looked out the window. Was he looking for something? I was very busy and soon forgot about him.

The next morning, at about seven o'clock, I was cooking eggs and making coffee for the officers. Suddenly, a handsome young black face arrived at the kitchen window. I looked at that face for a long time. The eggs burned. I couldn't move, because I knew! I took the young man's hands. I saw the old cut on his arm. I pushed his hair back and saw the other cut on his head.

"Boy!" I shouted. "You're my Henry! I've got you back again."

Oh, no, Mr. Clemens, I haven't had any trouble. And no happiness either!

Murder in Connecticut

I was feeling comfortable with my life. I lit a cigarette and picked up the morning's mail from the table in the hall. I was excited to see a letter from my favorite aunt. I always listened carefully to Aunt Mary. Most of her suggestions were excellent. But I didn't listen to her on the subject of cigarettes. When someone started talking about the dangers of smoking, I closed my ears. But I always welcomed the news of another visit from my aunt. She was coming that day!

I thought to myself: "I'm a happy man. If my worst enemy knocks at my door today, I will invite him into my house. I will love him and be his best friend."

My office door opened immediately. A fat, dirty, little green monster walked in. He was less than a meter tall and looked about forty years old. Every part of his body was a strange shape. He had bright, intelligent eyes, but they weren't friendly or kind. I looked closely at him. Why did I dislike this little man so much? He looked in many ways like me!

The monster sat down in my favorite chair. He put his dirty boots on my desk. Then he picked up my box of cigarettes.

"Give me a light!" the ugly little thing ordered.

My face turned red. Wasn't this *my* house? I was angry—and afraid, too. Where had this terrible thing come from?

"Listen," I said to the monster. "You are in *my* house. You must be polite to me, or I will throw you out of the window."

The *thing* smiled calmly and smoked his cigarette.

"Calm down. Don't give orders to a special guest," the monster said. Then he continued, "A visitor came to your door earlier today. Do you remember?"

"Of course I remember. Why is that your business?" I asked.

"It was a homeless man. He was hungry and asked for food. You lied to him and gave him nothing," the monster reported.

34

"Give me a light!" the ugly little thing ordered.

It was true. I sent the man away with nothing. Then, through the morning, I worried about my unkind actions.

"I told him—" I began.

"Wait! Stop! You're going to lie again. I know what you said. 'My wife has gone to the grocer's. I'm sorry, but there's no food in the house.' Two lies. Your wife was behind the door, and the cupboard was full of food.

"And what about yesterday?" the monster continued. "That young woman asked you to read her book. She wanted the opinion of a famous writer. You lied again. 'I have no time. Take your book to another writer.' She was crying when she left your house. The poor girl hid her book under her thin coat."

Why were my actions the business of this ugly green monster?

"You get angry with your children when they make a little noise," he continued. "You punish them for no reason. You forget about your old friends when they're sick or in need. You remember the bad things about people and forget the good ones. Are you kind and fair to your family and friends?"

"Why are you questioning me like this? Who *are* you?" I asked.

"I am your Conscience," said the monster.

"Really? This is good luck. I'm very pleased to meet you. But I'm sick of your speeches. You're always telling me what to do. If I kill you, I can forget about you," I said. "Isn't that right?"

My Conscience—the terrible little monster—jumped on top of my bookshelves. I threw some books at him, then a box, then a chair. I didn't hit him. He looked down and laughed at me.

"My friend, to murder me, you must be sorry for your bad thoughts and actions. Then I will grow big and heavy and will fall to the floor. But you aren't ashamed of yourself, so I am out of your reach. You can't catch me because I'm too light."

It was true. I wanted to feel sad and sorry, but I couldn't. I started to think. How could I kill my Conscience and forget about him?

Just then, the door opened and my son walked in.

"Father, why is this room in a mess?" asked the boy.

"Get out! Shut the door!" I shouted.

The boy hurried out of the room. I looked up at the monster.

"My son didn't see you, did he?" I said. "Why not?"

"No one can see me except you," explained the monster.

"Great!" I thought. "If I kill my Conscience, no one will know. No one can see him."

My bad thoughts made my Conscience even lighter. He was having trouble staying on his seat.

"Can I please ask you some questions?" I asked the monster, trying to seem friendly. "Why haven't I seen you before today?"

"Because today you wanted to be kind to your worst enemy. That's me," explained the monster.

"Let's be friends," I said. "Come down and smoke another cigarette with me."

"No, thanks. I'm not coming down. You want to kill me. I'm your enemy, not your friend. I rule you. Remember: I am your Conscience. You must follow my orders. Now, continue with your questions," the monster ordered.

"How long are you going to be here with me?"

"Always!" was the answer from the monster.

"But I don't want to see you and think about you every day."

"My dear boy," the monster began, "now I can look you straight in the eye. I can call you names. I can laugh at you. My job as your Conscience is much easier now."

This was terrible news. I had to kill him!

"Another question," I said. "Why do you tell me about my mistakes ten times? Tell me once and then be quiet."

"If you do something bad, of course I tell you about it again and again. It's my job—and I enjoy it," the monster said.

"But why do I have to suffer for days?" I asked. "You rob me of my true feelings. 'Why didn't you help that homeless man?' 'Why didn't you read that girl's book?' Too many questions!"

"Yes," the monster said, "I can always find something wrong with your thoughts and actions. I try my best."

"Don't worry—you miss nothing. You make me think about everything. Last Sunday I was in church, and the speaker asked for money for poor people. First, I thought about giving fifty dollars. Then I thought again and changed my gift to twenty. When the plate came around, I put in a dime. But when I got home, I was sorry about that dime. Then I heard your voice: 'Why didn't you give fifty dollars?'"

"That's very amusing. Tell me more," said the monster.

"Why should I talk to you? You're small and ugly and dirty. I'm glad that no one can see you. You're a mess."

"And who made me into a monster?" asked my Conscience.

"*I* don't know!" I answered.

"It was you. My looks are the result of your actions."

"Never! How did I make you into a monster?" I asked.

"When you were a boy of eight or nine, I was more than two meters high. I was strong, healthy, and good-looking."

"What happened to you?" I asked.

"You stopped listening to me. You began to do more bad things. Slowly, I became smaller and uglier. My skin became thicker and turned green. As I got weaker, I forgot to talk to you about some subjects, like smoking. Now, when you have a cigarette, I have a little sleep. But don't worry, I'll still talk to you about homeless people, young writers, and your children."

"What will happen if I do more bad things? If I stop listening to you, will you become smaller and quieter?" I asked.

"That's how it works," the monster agreed.

"I can make you disappear, can't I? Does that ever happen? Can I kill you by my bad actions?" I asked.

"It's possible. Some of my friends have died that way."

"Do you know a lot of consciences?" I asked.

"Yes, plenty of them. Everyone begins life with a conscience."

"Really? Can you describe my neighbor Mr. Thompson's conscience, please?"

"Yes, I met him when he was almost three meters tall. He had an excellent body and thick, beautiful hair. But things haven't gone well for Thompson. His conscience sleeps in a shoe box these days. He doesn't have a hair on his head."

"That sounds correct. Thompson is mean and selfish. Do you know Tom Smith's conscience?" I asked.

"Oh, yes. He was very small, like me, when he was two years old. But today he's ten meters tall. He has big, strong legs, clear eyes, and a handsome face. He never sleeps, really enjoys his job. He works night and day," the monster explained.

"Smith is the best man in this town," I agreed. "But he always wants to be better. Do you know my Aunt Mary's conscience?"

"I've seen her, but I haven't met her. She's very big. She lives in a field because no doorway is big enough for her."

"I can believe that. Aunt Mary isn't ashamed of her thoughts and actions," I said.

I heard a voice in the hall and opened the door. It was Aunt Mary. She hurried in with a lot of questions about my wife and children. Then she asked, "What has happened to that poor family around the corner? Have you kept your promise to help them?"

I looked up at my Conscience. My heavy heart was making him heavy, too. His head dropped down to his knees.

"Aunt Mary, I have been very busy. I'm writing—"

"No excuses, please. I'll do something for them tomorrow. Did you visit your old teacher last month?"

I turned red. My Conscience looked worried. He needed to stay light, to stay away from me.

"Dear Aunt," I began nervously, "I forgot that, too."

"Your teacher died last week, completely alone, without a friend in the world. Are you ashamed of yourself?"

I *was* ashamed. Under the weight of my suffering, my Conscience fell to the floor. He lay there, wanting to get away. He knew he was in real danger.

Suddenly, I had a plan. I ran to the door and locked it.

"What's the matter?" asked Aunt Mary. "Have you gone crazy? Why are you looking at that place on the floor?"

"I'm a little nervous, Aunt. It's because I smoke too much."

"Promise me that you will throw out your pipe and cigarettes."

My Conscience was trying to move toward the door but became heavier with every one of Aunt Mary's words. I watched the little monster carefully. When he closed his eyes, I jumped on him. I took him by his neck and pulled him to pieces. At last, and forever, my Conscience was dead. I was a free man!

I shouted at my aunt, "No more speeches about smoking, please. No more little talks about right and wrong. My ears are closed and my heart is dead. I am a man without a conscience."

Aunt Mary ran out of my house.

What did I do after that day? I murdered thirty-eight people in the first two weeks—people I hated for their past actions. I burned down a house that blocked my view. I stole from the rich and the poor and kept everything for myself. I didn't worry about my crimes, because my Conscience was dead.

What about the future? I think it looks bright. I enjoy a bottle of fine wine and a few cigarettes in the evening. Then I go to bed and sleep very well. I wake up with new plans. There is no questioning voice in my head. In fact, there are no voices around me. I'm alone in the house and have no visitors. So, I will always be my own boss. It's the best way, don't you agree?

Ed Jackson Meets Cornelius Vanderbilt

In the 1850s, Memphis, Tennessee was ready to become the center of the tobacco business along the east coast of America. Smart businessmen noticed the signs, so they started to prepare. They began to buy boats to move the tobacco. They found honest men to work for them. Then they waited for the tobacco business to grow. But at first, there wasn't much tobacco traffic along the river. This meant a lot of free time for the strong, young workers. These men didn't want to sit around all day with nothing to do. So they amused themselves by playing practical jokes on their friends.

It was easy to trick Ed Jackson. He believed every wild story that the other workers told him. He also laughed at himself and never stayed angry with the practical jokers.

One day, Ed told his friends about his vacation plans. He was not going fishing as usual. This summer, he had a better plan. He had forty dollars in a box under his bed, and he wanted to visit New York City.

It was a surprising idea. It meant real travel in those days. To the workmen, it meant seeing the world. At first, Ed's friends didn't believe him. But when he continued to make his plans, they started planning, too. They could play a wonderful practical joke on Ed—something really funny.

The young men discussed many ideas. Then they held a secret meeting and chose the best one. It was wonderful! It was big and exciting! It was perfect!

"We'll give him a letter to carry to Mr. Cornelius Vanderbilt, the richest businessman in the United States," explained Charley Fairchild. "It will be from my father to his old school friend, Mr. Vanderbilt."

41

"Did your father really go to school with that famous millionaire?" asked Robert Parker.

"No, of course not!" Charley answered. "Listen carefully. In the letter, my father will introduce Ed to old Vanderbilt. But Mr. Vanderbilt has never met my dad. He'll throw Ed out of his office."

"Do you think Ed will forgive us? Will he understand that it's a joke?" asked Robert.

"Maybe he'll get really mad. Then he'll come back and kill us," suggested Tim Bailey.

"But it's a great practical joke," Charley said. "We have to try it."

The friends all agreed with Charley Fairchild and began to work on the letter. It was prepared very carefully, in a simple, friendly style.

The letter said:

The holder of this letter is a very close friend of my dear son. He is kind, brave, and honest. As an old friend, I ask you to be good to this young man.

It has been a long time since we were boys. Do you remember all of our good times together as schoolboys? I have many wonderful memories of adventures with you. Remember when we stole some apples from old Mr. Stevenson's yard? He ran after us, but we were young and fast. We sold his own apples to his cook later that day. We had so many good times. Do you remember . . .

The letter continued with more amusing stories. Then it was signed:

from your old friend Alfred Fairchild

Charley found Ed at the river the next day.

"Ed," Charley began, "would you like a letter of introduction to Mr. Cornelius Vanderbilt? You know, he lives in New York City."

"What? You don't know him, do you?" Ed asked.

"No, but my father does. They were schoolboys together. If you want a letter, I'll ask my father. I'm sure he'll write something for you."

Ed was very grateful and pleased with this offer. Three days passed, and the letter was put into his hands. He left his friends, repeating his thanks. When Ed was gone, the other workmen laughed about their trick. But then they began to worry. Ed was their friend. They didn't want him to hate them for this wonderful practical joke.

Ed Jackson arrived in New York City and went straight to Mr. Cornelius Vanderbilt's offices. He sat in the large waiting room with about twenty other people. Everyone wanted a word with the millionaire in his private office. The secretary asked for Ed's card; he gave her the letter from Mr. Fairchild. Ed's name was called almost immediately. He went into a big office and found Mr. Vanderbilt alone with the letter in his hand.

"Please, sit down, Mr. Jackson."

"Thank you, sir," Ed said nervously.

"I see from the first sentence of this letter that it's from an old friend. Now, what's his name?" Mr. Vanderbilt said. He turned the letter over and found the signature. "Oh, yes, Alfred Fairchild. I don't remember that name. But that means nothing—I've forgotten thousands of names. He says—he says—oh, yes—something about *apples*. Oh, that's good. I don't quite remember it, but maybe . . . Oh, and a game we played together. Oh, yes, wonderful! It brings back memories. It's a long time ago. I can't remember all of the names. But, it all feels right! We were happy boys. The memories warm my heart.

"But people are waiting. I'll keep the rest of the letter for tonight. I'll enjoy it at home. Please thank Mr. Fairchild for me. I called him *Alf*, I think. I feel young when I think of dear Alf. Tell him I'll help him or a friend of his any time.

"And you, young man, will be my guest. You can't stay at a

hotel in New York. Wait for me outside and we'll go home together. You'll have a wonderful time. No worries about that."

Ed stayed a week in New York City and had a great vacation. He didn't realize that Mr. Vanderbilt was watching him. By the end of the visit, the millionaire was very pleased with Ed. In fact, the great businessman was thinking about the tobacco business in Memphis. He wanted to discuss this with Ed before he returned to Tennessee.

"My young friend," Mr. Vanderbilt began, "you're going home tomorrow. But first we must talk about tobacco. I want to open a tobacco business in Memphis, and I want you to run it. I've watched you for a week. You're the best man for the job."

"*Me!*" replied Ed. This was a surprise.

"Yes. You will have to work hard, but I will pay you well. Find the best men to work for you. You'll be the boss. You'll report only to me."

After talking about the business plans, Mr. Vanderbilt said, "Goodbye, my boy. Thank Alf for sending you to me."

When Ed reached Memphis, he hurried down to the river. He wanted to tell his friends everything about New York City, about Mr. Cornelius Vanderbilt, and about his new job. It was a very hot day and no one seemed to be around. Then Ed saw Charley Fairchild, sleeping on an old chair. Ed touched Charley's shoulder and woke him up. Charley saw Ed, jumped up, and ran away.

Ed didn't understand. Was Charley crazy? He walked toward the river and saw two more of his friends. They were talking and laughing. But, like Charley, they ran off when they saw Ed. What was happening?

Then Ed saw Robert Parker on one of the boats. When Robert saw Ed, he jumped into the water.

"I didn't do it," shouted Robert from the water.

"Didn't do *what*?" Ed asked.

"Give you the—"

"I didn't do it."

"Forget the past. Come out of the water. What have *I* done?" shouted Ed.

"You? Nothing. But are you angry with any of us?" Robert asked.

"Of course not. Should I be?"

"Maybe not. Will you shake my hand?" asked Robert.

"I'd love to," Ed replied. "I want to shake someone's hand before they run off."

The other men came back when they saw Ed and Robert together. Each man thought: "Maybe he lost the letter. Maybe he forgot about it." Now they wanted to know all about Ed's trip.

"Well, when I gave Mr. Vanderbilt the letter—" Ed began.

"What? You met Cornelius Vanderbilt?" asked Tim Bailey.

"*Did* you give him the letter?" asked Charley Fairchild.

The men were feeling a little nervous. Then they listened to Ed's wonderful story and began to smile. When Ed finished, he said, "Boys, you're the greatest friends in the world. You're big jokers, but you're the best. I'm going to give you all good jobs in Mr. Vanderbilt's Memphis tobacco company. And Charley, you will be my first assistant because you got me the letter. You and your father changed my life. Now, let's drink to that great man: Mr. Cornelius Vanderbilt. And, I'm buying!"

Yes, when the time is right, the right man comes. Even if he arrives there because of a practical joke.

A Dog's Life

My father was a big St. Bernard.★ My mother was a collie.★ Mother was famous because she loved long, difficult words. The other dogs in the neighborhood thought she was really smart.

Sometimes Mother sat at the school window and listened to the children's lessons. When she heard a big word, she repeated it to herself. Then she used it with a group of dogs. Sometimes a new dog was surprised and asked, "What does that word mean?" Mother always answered the question immediately. This surprised the stranger even more.

Of course, no one questioned Mother about her explanations. To the other dogs, she sounded like a page from a dictionary. When I was older, Mother brought home the word *romantic*. She used that word again and again with different groups of dogs. Everyone was excited about this excellent new word. I listened carefully for about a week. Mother calmly explained *romantic* in eight different ways on eight different days.

Mother liked to listen to Mr. Thompson, our owner, and his guests. The men often told jokes after dinner, and laughed at the good ones. Sometimes, Mother brought home the men's jokes. She knew the beginnings of the jokes, but she never remembered the end. This didn't worry her. She finished a joke her way, and then lay on her back and laughed. The other dogs lay on their backs and laughed, too. They didn't understand the joke, but they didn't want to seem stupid.

You can see that my mother wasn't always honest. But she was very popular and good in other ways. She had a kind heart, and she tried to help anyone in need. She told her children, "Do not run away from danger. If a friend or a stranger is in trouble, help

★ St. Bernard; collie: types of dog

47

him. Don't worry about the cost to yourself." She taught us this by words and by example. She was a real soldier.

When I was one year old, I was sold. On my last day with her, Mother kissed me and said, "Aileen, my daughter, we have a purpose in this life. We must help others when we can. This will make our lives on Earth good and happy." This was a lesson from her visits to the children's school, and she believed it. Do you think I could forget my mother's words? No. Never.

My new house was a beautiful, happy home! It had handsome furniture and expensive pictures. There was also a big yard with old trees and flowers everywhere! I was part of the family.

Mrs. Gray was thirty years old, a sweet mother and a loving wife. Sadie was ten and just like her mother, with a pretty face and long brown hair. The baby was a year old and quite fat. He loved to hold my tail for a ride around the living room. Mr. Gray was thirty-eight, tall, and handsome. He was a famous scientist (a good word for my mother). Every week, a group of scientists joined Mr. Gray in his laboratory (another one for Mother). They used his machines and discussed big ideas. I was sorry that I couldn't understand very much of their conversations.

Other times, I slept on the floor of Mrs. Gray's workroom or played with the children. The cooks and other workers in our house were all kind to me, too. I was the happiest dog on Earth and very grateful for a good home. Each day, I thought about my mother. I remembered her words and tried to do the right thing.

I was even happier when my little son was born. He was the dearest, prettiest little dog in the world. He had a sweet face and loving eyes. Sadie named him Robin after his father.

One winter day, I was in the baby's bedroom. I was guarding the baby while his nurse was in the kitchen. I was asleep on the floor, and the baby was asleep in his little bed. A large fire kept us warm and comfortable. Suddenly, the baby's scream woke me. His bed was on fire. I ran toward the door, but in a second I saw my

Suddenly, the baby's scream woke me. His bed was on fire.

mother's face, and I ran back to the baby's bed. I reached through the fire and took the baby's clothes in my teeth. We fell to the floor together in a cloud of smoke. I pulled the screaming baby along the floor and into the hall. Then I heard Mr. Gray's loud voice.

"Aileen, drop that child! You terrible, terrible animal!"

I jumped away from the baby. Mr. Gray ran after me. He hit me very hard with his stick. He only stopped when the nurse shouted, "Sir, the baby's room is on fire!"

The pain in my legs and back was very bad. I walked slowly on three legs. One leg was broken, and I was afraid of Mr. Gray and his stick. I hid in a dark closet in an old part of the house, behind some old furniture. I kept very quiet in my secret place. I wanted to cry because of the pain, but I didn't.

I could hear noise from other parts of the house. After a long time, I fell asleep. The next day, I woke up and made a plan. I thought: "I will leave the house in the middle of the night. I will escape from Mr. Gray and his stick." Then I remembered: "I can't leave this house. I can't leave my little Robin."

I had to stay in the closet and wait. I heard everyone calling my name, but I was afraid. Did Mr. Gray want to hit me again?

I stayed in the closet for days, very hungry and thirsty. I was also getting very weak, and I slept a lot of the time. But I woke one day when I heard Sadie's sweet voice.

"Aileen! Come back to us, please. Forgive my father. We are so sad without you. Robin misses you."

I made a grateful little sound. The next minute, Sadie was next to me. "Aileen's found! She's here!" she shouted.

The following days were perfect. Mrs. Gray made me a soft bed in her workroom, and I was given the best food from the kitchen. Every day, friends and neighbors came to hear my story.

"Aileen saved the baby's life," explained Mrs. Gray.

Everyone spoke nicely to me. They said, "She is the best and bravest dog in the world."

"What happened to her leg?" visitors sometimes asked. But Sadie and Mrs. Gray looked ashamed and didn't answer this question.

Soon I had a bigger surprise. Mr. Gray brought twenty of his scientist friends to see me. They looked at me for a long time. Then they discussed me very seriously.

"She is wonderful for a dumb animal. She saved your child. Of course, she didn't think. She didn't know what she was doing," one of the scientists said.

"No, you're wrong!" shouted Mr. Gray. "She understood exactly how to save the baby. She can think and understand better than many men and women."

The scientists discussed me for hours. Then they changed to another interesting subject: blindness. I knew a blind dog in the neighborhood and wanted to hear the scientists' opinions on this subject. Some people are blind when they are born. Others become blind after an accident or an illness. They decided to do tests on different kinds of blindness. They wanted to discover the reasons for this problem.

The men also discussed plants. This subject interested me because each spring, Sadie planted flowers. We watched them grow in the summer. I wanted to tell the men about Sadie's flowers, but I couldn't, and soon they were talking about blindness again. I became bored and fell asleep.

The following spring, Mrs. Gray and the children went to the coast to visit Mrs. Gray's younger sister. I was happy to play with Robin in the fresh air. But we were counting the days until the children and Mrs. Gray returned.

One day, the group of scientists came back. Mr. Gray took my son into his laboratory with the men. I was pleased that my little Robin was interesting to these important people. I sat outside of the window and waited for him.

Suddenly, I heard Robin scream in pain. I looked in the window and saw him. His head was covered in blood. Mr. Gray put my little son on the floor, but he couldn't walk in a straight line.

"There!" shouted Mr. Gray. "I've won. He's completely blind. The test has proved my idea."

All the men said, "Good work! This important result will help many people."

As the scientists shook Mr. Gray's hand, they forgot about little Robin. He lay in a corner, crying softly. I ran inside, went to him, and made him comfortable. He put his head against mine, though he couldn't see me. I knew that he was happy at his mother's touch. Then his head dropped to the floor. He didn't move or make a sound.

Mr. Gray walked over to us. He called one of the workmen. "Put him in a hole in the ground under the big apple tree."

I followed the workman into the yard. I thought, "Robin will grow in the ground. I will see him in the summer. He will be a fine, handsome dog like his father, and a wonderful surprise for the children."

When the workman finished his job, he turned to me. There were tears in his eyes. "Poor dog. You saved *his* child."

I have watched the place under the apple tree for two weeks, but Robin hasn't come up! I think something terrible has happened. This fear makes me sick. I can't eat. I cry at night. Every day, I grow weaker. When I closed my eyes this evening, I heard two workmen talking.

"Poor children! They don't know about their pets. They'll come home tomorrow morning and ask for little Robin and for Aileen. Who will be strong enough to tell them the true story? Their two brave, good friends have gone. They're in a better world now."

ACTIVITIES

"Jim Smiley and His Jumping Frog" and "The Other Side of War"

Before you read

1 Read the Introduction to this book. Which of these statements are incorrect?
   a Mark Twain was his real name.
   b He was born in the 1830s.
   c He lived near the Mississippi River.
   d He did a number of different jobs.
   e He never left the United States.
   f He was a poor man when he died.

2 Look at the Word List at the back of this book. Complete these sentences with words from the list.
   a The ... worked all day in the fields, picking ... . They were paid nothing, of course.
   b I drove up from Mexico City to the U.S. ... . But I didn't have a ..., so I had to return home.
   c He was a famous ... . Then he lost all his money ... on horses.
   d The ... was killed when one of his own soldiers accidentally ... his gun.
   e I often played ... on my sister. Once I put a ... in her bed. It jumped out when she pulled back the top sheet.

While you read

3 In "Jim Smiley and His Jumping Frog," what kind of animal are these?
   a the fifteen-minute racer ....
   b Andrew Jackson ....
   c Daniel Webster ....
   d Betsy Ross ....
   Now name these animals.
   e It has one eye and no tail. ....
   f It is old, thin, and coughs a lot. ....
   g It dies after losing a fight. ....
   h Jim Smiley teaches it to jump. ....

54

4 Complete the list of places in "The Other Side of War" where the young soldiers stop between the beginning and end of their trip in Hannibal, Missouri.

  a On the first night, they form a circle around

     a .... near New

     ....

  b On the second day, they have breakfast and hear a speech at

     ....

  c For a few days, they sleep in an old empty farm near

     ....

  d After news about enemy soldiers, they hurry back to

     .... and are attacked by dogs.

  e After more news about Union soldiers, they hide in

     ....

  f The next morning, they hurry back to

     .... for breakfast and stay for a

     week.

  g After fresh news of enemy soldiers, they return to

     ....

  Finally, they decide to go home to Hannibal, Missouri.

After you read

5 Why are these people and things important to the story of

  a "Jim Smiley and His Jumping Frog"?

Simon Wheeler	Leonidas W. Smiley
the fifteen-minute racer	a dog with no back legs
forty dollars	sand

  b "The Other Side of War"?

    The Hannibal Confederate Company

Tom Lyman	Joe Smith
General Ralls	Jeb Mason's farm
General Tom Harris	

6 Work with another student. Have one of these conversations.

   a *Student A:*   You are the storyteller of "Jim Smiley and His Jumping Frog." Talk to the friend who suggested speaking to Simon Wheeler. What did you think of your visit to Calaveras?

      Student B: You are the storyteller's friend. Ask questions about this visit to Calaveras. Tell him or her why you suggested the visit.

   b *Student A:*   You are the storyteller of "The Other Side of War." You have returned home. Tell your mother what happened.

      Student B: You are the storyteller's mother. Ask your son questions. Tell him what you think of his actions.

"Is He Living or Is He Dead?" and "Passport to Russia"

Before you read

   7 Who is your favorite painter? Describe his or her paintings.

   8 How is a passport different from a visa? Why is a passport important?

While you read

   9 Put these actions in the correct order.

     "Is He Living or Is He Dead?" (1–6)

     a The world reads about the death of Millet.   .....

     b Carl Boulander suggests a plan that will save the four artists.   .....

     c The four artists become millionaires.   .....

     d Mr. Smith and François Millet (as Théophile Magnan) visit Mentone.   .....

     e Carl sells the *Angelus* for 2,200 francs.   .....

     f Three of the young artists travel around France with news that François Millet is very sick.   .....

     "Passport to Russia" (1–6)

     g Professor Jackson leaves Parrish's passport at the Russian consulate.   .....

h Professor Jackson goes to the ticket office in
Berlin.   .....

i Alfred Parrish meets the secretary of the
American consulate.   .....

j Alfred Parrish drinks a beer with some American
college students.   .....

k Parrish and Professor Jackson cross the border
into Russia.   .....

l Alfred Parrish leaves the bar without paying his bill.   .....

After you read

10 What happens next?

"Is He Living or Is He Dead?"

a Mr. Smith asks the storyteller, "Do you know any of Hans
Andersen's stories?"

b The storyteller, Claude Frère, and Carl Boulander arrive in a
small northern town in France.

c After two years together, the four artists have no money and no
food.

d The storyteller, Claude, and Carl travel around France.

e Mr. Smith finishes his story about the four artists.

"Passport to Russia"

f Alfred Parrish puts his last bank note on the table in the Berlin
bar.

g Professor Jackson and Alfred Parrish take a taxi to the Russian
consulate in Berlin.

h Professor Jackson and Alfred arrive at the Russian border.

i Professor Jackson and Alfred visit Prince Bossloffsky.

j The secretary at the American consulate learns Alfred Parrish's
name.

11 Choose one of the two stories. Tell the story, in your own words,
to a group of other students. Then answer any questions that they
have.

"A True Story" and "Murder in Connecticut"

Before you read

12 Find some facts about the use of slaves in the United States. Look in books or on the Internet. When were slaves used? Who were they? Where were they from?

13 Discuss this question with other students: Should you always listen to your conscience? Do you? Why (not)?

While you read

14 Who:

"A True Story"

a works for Mr. Clemens and his family? ....

b owns Aunt Rachel when she is 18? ....

c call themselves old Blue Chickens? ....

d owns Aunt Rachel before the Civil War? ....

e finds his mother after 13 years? ....

"Murder in Connecticut"

f is the storyteller's favorite aunt? ....

g does the little monster look like? ....

h are two people that the storyteller lies to? ....

i is the storyteller's worst enemy? ....

j is the best man in town? ....

k is living alone at the end of the story? ....

After you read

15 Are these sentences right (✓) or wrong (✗)?

"A True Story"

a Aunt Rachel always seems happy to Mr. Clemens. .....

b Aunt Rachel marries a bad man. .....

c Aunt Rachel tries to protect Henry in Richmond. .....

d The polite Union officers know Rachel's son. .....

e Henry is a good dancer. .....

f Aunt Rachel's story has a happy ending. .....

"Murder in Connecticut"

g The storyteller isn't a smoker. .....

h The storyteller wants to murder his conscience.   .....
i The storyteller's son looks carefully at his
   father's conscience.   .....
j The monster likes his job.   .....
k Good people have very small consciences.   .....
l Without a conscience, the storyteller becomes
   a bad person.   .....

16 Compare the two stories. Are they funny or sad? Are the people in them rich or poor? How many differences can you think of? Which story did you like more?

"Ed Jackson Meets Cornelius Vanderbilt" and "A Dog's Life"

Before you read

17 Which sentences do you agree with? Discuss your answers with other students.

   a Practical jokes are always a lot of fun for everyone.
   b People with a lot of money are not very nice.
   c It is acceptable for scientists to use animals for their tests.
   d Animals understand what people say.

While you read

18 Circle the correct word.

   "Ed Jackson Meets Cornelius Vanderbilt"

   a Ed's *friends / enemies* like to play practical jokes on him.
   b Ed has *fourteen / forty* dollars for a trip to New York City.
   c Alfred Fairchild *is / isn't* an old friend of Cornelius Vanderbilt's.
   d In New York, Ed stays at *Mr. Vanderbilt's house / a cheap hotel*.
   e Ed has a *wonderful / terrible* time in New York City.
   f Cornelius Vanderbilt wants Ed to run his tobacco business in *New York / Tennessee*.
   g Ed asks *Tim Bailey / Charley Fairchild* to be his first assistant.

   "A Dog's Life"

   h The other dogs think that Aileen's mother is very *stupid / smart*.
   i Aileen lives with her mother for *a short time / a very long time*.

j Aileen is *happy/unhappy* with the Gray family before the fire in the baby's room.

k Aileen saves *Robin's/the baby's* life.

l *Mrs. Gray/Sadie* finds Aileen in the dark closet.

m Mr. Gray's test makes *Aileen/Robin* blind.

After you read

19 Which of these people or animals from the two stories do you like? Discuss your reasons with other students.

    a Cornelius Vanderbilt, Charley Fairchild, Ed Jackson

    b Aileen's mother, Sadie Gray, Mr. Gray, Robin, Aileen

20 Complete these sentences.

    a Cornelius Vanderbilt happily meets Ed Jackson because …

    b Mr. Vanderbilt gives Ed a job because …

    c After his trip, Ed's friends stay away from him because …

    d Aileen hides in the closet because …

    e Mr. Gray and the scientists use Robin in a test because …

    f Aileen dies because …

21 One of these two stories has a happy ending and the other has a sad ending. What changes are necessary for Ed Jackson's story to end sadly? How must Aileen's story change to end happily?

Writing

22 Write the story that Simon Wheeler starts at the end of "Jim Smiley and His Jumping Frog." The story begins: "Smiley had a yellow cat with one eye and no tail. This cat's name was Betsy Ross, and …"

23 Write a conversation between Tom Lyman and his grandson. Begin the conversation with the grandson's question: "Grandpa, what did you do in the Civil War?"

24 You are one of the four young artists in "Is He Living or Is He Dead?" Write a report for an English newspaper about the death of François Millet. You want people to become interested in buying Millet's paintings.

25 You are Alfred Parrish. You are back in the United States for your final year in college. Write a short paper about your time in Europe: "My Summer Vacation."

26 It is twenty years after "A True Story" and Aunt Rachel has just died. Write a short speech about her life for Mr. Clemens to give at the church service.

27 The storyteller describes his Conscience in "Murder in Connecticut." Write a description of *your* Conscience.

28 You are Ed Jackson. Write a thank-you letter to Mr. Cornelius Vanderbilt for your vacation and for your new job. Describe your favorite parts of your visit to New York City. Tell him how successful the new tobacco company is.

29 You are Sadie Gray. When you return from the coast, you learn that Robin and Aileen are dead. Write a short poem about one of them.

30 You want to make a movie for TV of one of Mark Twain's short stories. Choose a story and give the television company a list of reasons for making this program.

31 Which person in these stories would you like to meet? Write about him or her and explain why.

WORD LIST

ashamed (adj) feeling bad, not proud, about something you have done

bet (v) to try to win money by guessing the result of something, like a race or a game

blind (adj) unable to see

border (n) the line where two countries meet

chain (n) metal rings joined in a line

conscience (n) a voice inside a person's head that tells him or her about right and wrong

consul (n) a government officer, living in a foreign city. The consul helps people from his or her country. The consul's office is called a consulate.

fire (v) to shoot a gun

frog (n) a small green animal with long legs that lives near water

general (n) an officer with the highest position for a soldier

homesick (adj) feeling sad because you are a long way from your home

laboratory (n) a room or building in which scientists do tests

leader (n) the person that other people follow and take orders from

millionaire (n) a very rich person who has one million dollars or more

monster (n) an ugly, scary person or animal in stories

practical joke (n) a trick that is used to surprise someone. It is amusing to other people.

slave (n) someone who is owned by another person. Slaves work for their owners without pay.

tobacco (n) a dried plant used for making cigarettes

uniform (n) a type of clothes worn by people in the same company, club, or other organization

visa (n) a stamp in your passport that lets you go into or out of another country

The Black Cat and Other Stories
Edgar Allan Poe

These four stories of murder and mystery will frighten you! Edgar Allan Poe writes about terrible people with strange lives. Do you have a black cat . . . ?

The Three Adventures of Sherlock Holmes
Sir Arthur Conan Doyle

Sherlock Holmes is a great detective. There are few cases that he cannot solve. In these three stories we meet a young woman who is very frightened of a 'speckled band', a family who think that five orange pips are a sign of death, and banker who believes that his son is a thief. But are things really as they seem?

The Canterbury Tales
Geoffrey Chaucer

A group of pilgrims travel together from London to Canterbury. Each pilgrim has to tell a story to keep the others amused. These fourteenth-century stories show how little human nature has changed.